HOW TO SMILE WHEN EVERYTHING GOES DEAD WRONG

50 YEARS AS AN NHS NURSE

BARBARA PICKERSGILL

Copyright © 2018 Barbara Pickersgill

This is a limited edition, produced for the friends & family of the author

Published by Barbara Pickersgill

Edited & designed by
Book of My Life Ltd
20 Clyde Terrace
London
SE23 3BA
020 8133 6588
bookofmylife.co.uk

Book of My Life

For Lisa, my daughter

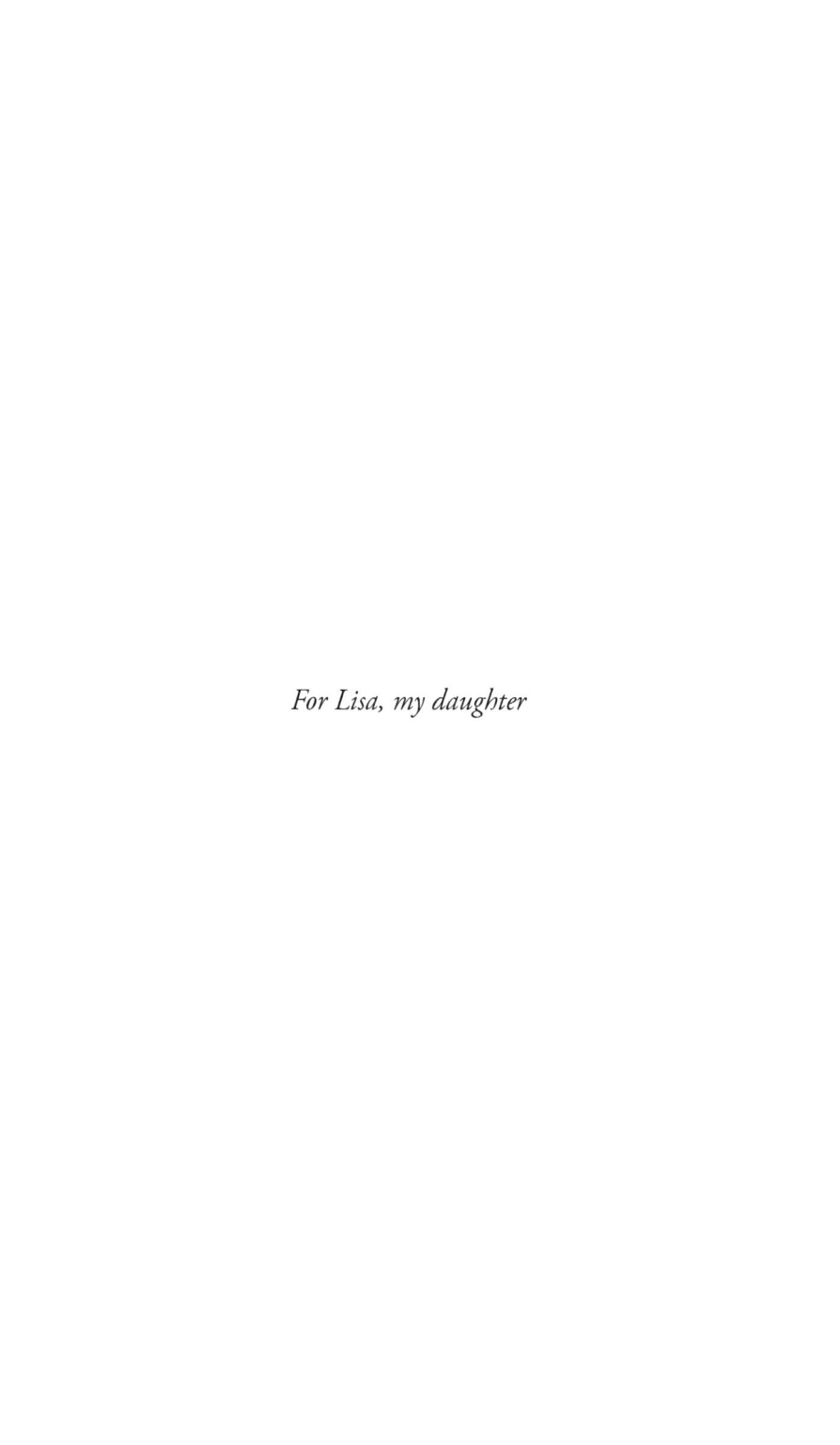

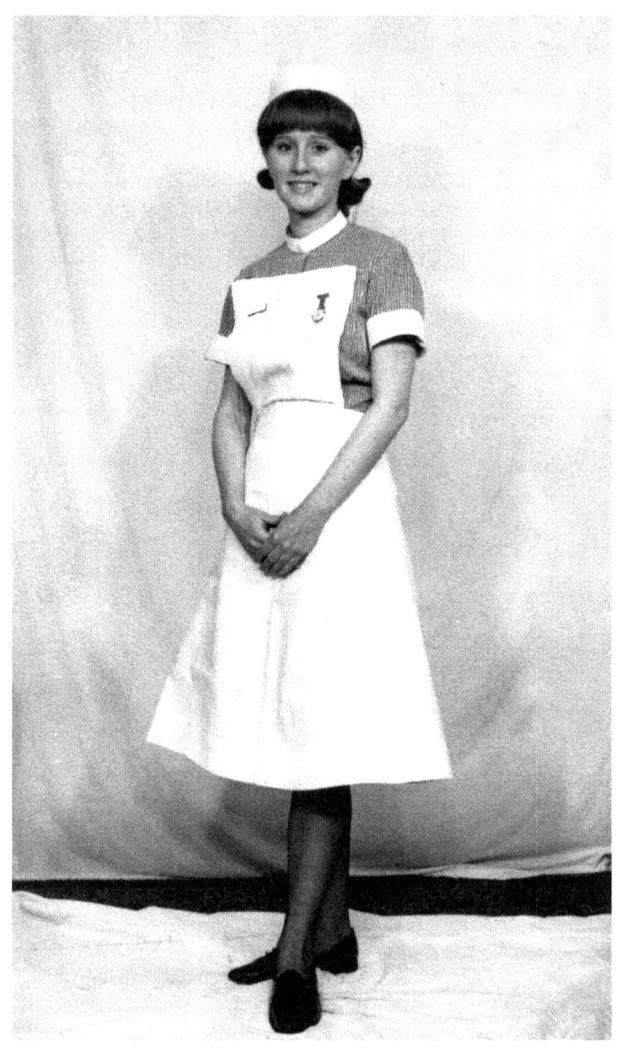

Me, Barbara Pickersgill (née Padgett), at the start of my registration training, 1964–1967

Preface

I wrote this book because I wanted to leave a legacy for my family and friends. It shows my journey through the years of my nursing career—50 in total! The photographs were mostly taken by me, or my colleagues, as they happened. They show the many changes in the NHS during the decades when I worked there.

Clayton Hospital, Wakefield

I
Leaving School

I left school at 16 after a modest secondary education. I had failed my 11-plus examination but had a desire to join the police force.

My parents, my sister and I lived in a mining village called Fitzwilliam in West Yorkshire. My father was a miner, as were most of the men in the village. In fact, the village had been named after the family who owned the local colliery.

My parents supported my ambition to join the police force. They arranged for me to take an entrance examination at police-cadet training school in Sheffield. I passed the exam and was given a place on a training course for policewomen. Unfortunately, I was told that I couldn't start the training until I was 18. I would have to wait another two years.

In the meantime, I took a job in a sewing factory in my village. After six months there, I was not happy. I yearned for a more interesting, and useful, job. My grandma was a nurse, and my mother encouraged me to think about a career in nursing, following in my grandma's footsteps.

My father arranged an interview with the matron at Clayton Hospital in Wakefield, which had its own nurse-training school. My mother accompanied me to my interview. Matron was polite (I was petrified), although she was a typical matron—very upright and to the point.

"As you failed your 11-plus, and only had a secondary modern education, you might struggle with the training," she said.

She could see that I was disappointed. Happily, she then said that she was willing to give me a chance. She suggested I start the cadet-nursing course, which would take me up to the age of 18. Then I could start my SRN (State Registered Nurse) training.

I was over the moon and was really looking forward to starting. Of course, I still had my place at police college to fall back on if I didn't like nursing.

One month later I began cadet-nurse training at Clayton Hospital.

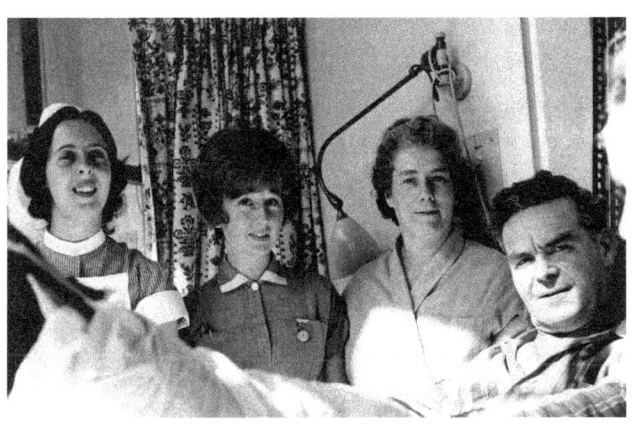

Cadet training, 1963–1964. On the orthopaedic ward G2, Clayton Hospital in 1963

II
A Cadet Nurse

The cadet course was 18 months long. This would take me up to my 18th birthday.

But when I started I was just 16 and very shy. The course involved two days a week at Wakefield College studying anatomy and physiology plus hygiene. The other three days I was working on the hospital wards, which were extremely busy.

The patients were varied and all interesting. They kept telling me I was too young to be a nurse.

Some of the patients on the orthopaedic ward stayed for many months. For example, patients with fractured femurs were attached to a splint pulley which had to be adjusted each day, and they had to remain in bed for three months.

These were young men, and bored, with no television on the ward, no mobile phones nor Internet—not like today!

The wards contained patients with different conditions: orthopaedic on one side, surgical and medical on the other.

In general, the wards were large and open, each with 30 beds. One had a four-bed cubicle in which to nurse ophthalmic patients having eye surgery. They needed a quiet environment to aid their recovery.

I was enjoying my cadet training, helping with feeding patients, chatting to the staff and patients. I was learning a lot at the college and was able to relate it to my practical experience on the wards.

I worked on all the wards in the hospital, but the one I enjoyed working on most was the children's ward. I spent a lot of time amusing the children before and after they had surgery.

Nursing was definitely for me. I enjoyed every minute of it and could not wait to start my SRN training.

The 18 months' cadet training went by quickly and I passed all my exams. Now I was ready to do this properly. My parents were keen for me to continue with a nursing career and did all they could to encourage me, even driving me to hospital each day and later setting me up in the hospital's nurses' home.

Outside ACI ward, Clayton Hospital

In the gardens with patients at Clayton Hospital, 1963

Next page: at Harrogate nurse training centre, 1964
for a three-month induction to nursing

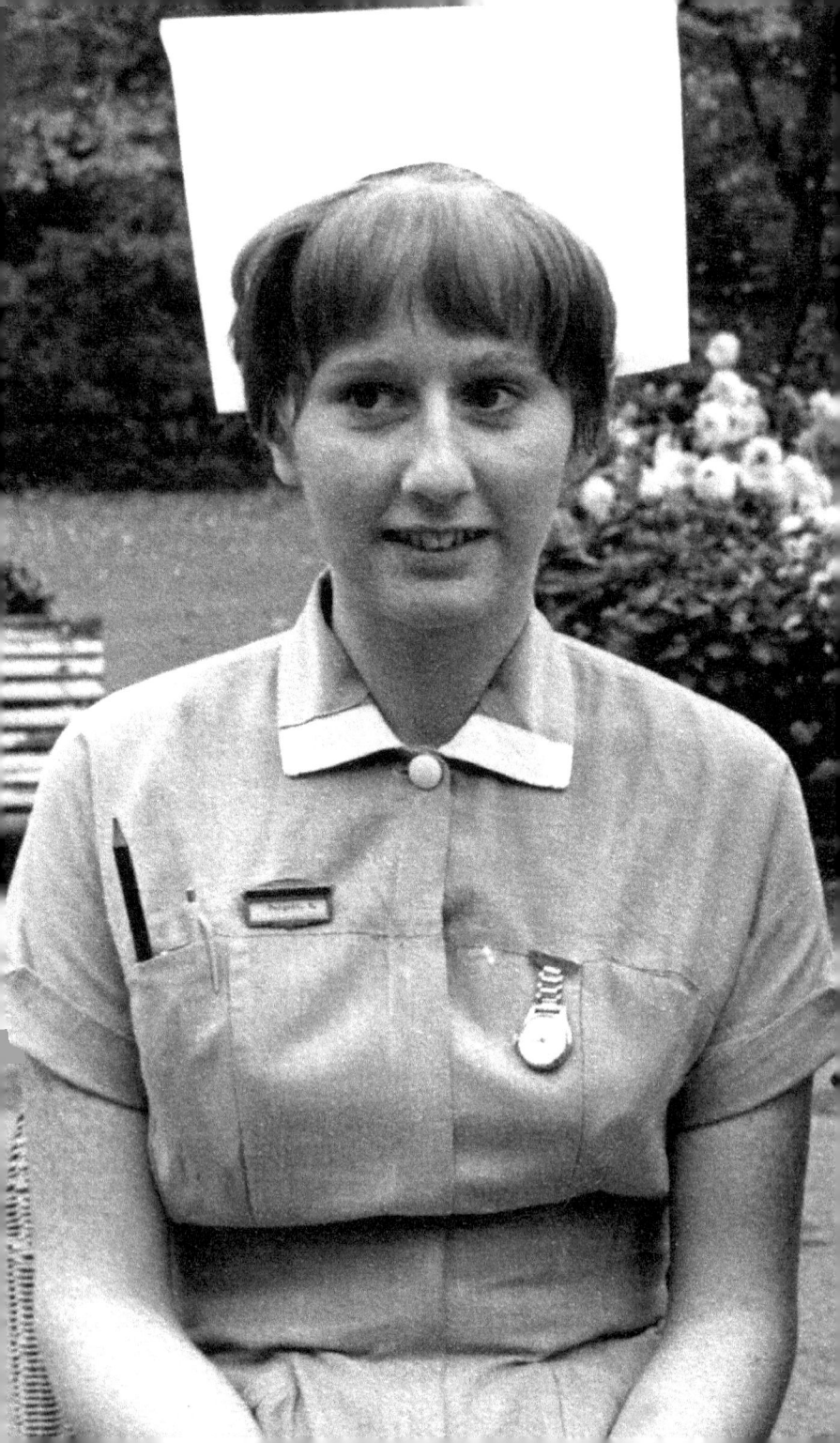

III
SRN Training

My official start date for my three-year nurse training at Clayton Hospital was 20 April 1964. My salary would be £8 per week, and I was granted three weeks' annual leave.

During the first year, I was required to live at the hospital and was given a room in the hospital nurses' home. This was the first time I had been away from home, but I was 18 and feeling very grown up!

The first three months of the training (induction) were spent at Harrogate School of Nursing. I would work for a week at Harrogate then come home at weekends on the train.

It was during these three months that I met the love of my life, my husband John. John's parents were farmers, and John worked long hours on the family farm. My sister set me up on a date with John—a blind date in fact. This turned into a lifetime together. (We've now been married for 50 years.) John had a small A40 van and drove me back to Harrogate each weekend.

The three months at Harrogate Nursing School soon passed, and I was back at Clayton Hospital to continue my training.

I had to visit the sewing room to be fitted with the uniform and be shown how to fold the special nurses' hats. Now I felt like a real nurse! There were ten girls on my course, and I was the best at folding the hats. I always folded all the other girls' hats for them!

In the hospital's training school we had all our practical experience, often practising on each other.

We were also taught all the theory in the training school from tutors, doctors and consultants. When not in school, we had practical placements on the wards: children's, ACI/ACII, surgical, medical, Hannah Pickard, orthopaedic GP, obstetrics and outpatients.

Each placement was for six weeks, which meant that we had good experience of all the wards.

The training school was extremely well equipped and the tutors were excellent—a bit scary but highly professional.

It is different today. Most of the nursing course is taught in a university with very little practical experience until the last year of training.

Outside nursing accommodation at Clayton Hospital. My room is above my head

Working on the Wards

Matron carried out her ward rounds on all the wards twice a day—quite a task.

The ward sister would be busy preparing for Matron's visit when we'd hear the sound of footsteps coming along the corridor.

"Oh no," we'd all say, "it's Matron!"

We'd all run into the sluice room to hide. We knew that Matron would choose a student nurse to take on the ward round and none of us wanted to be picked.

Standing at the bottom of the patient's bed, the student nurse was expected to know the name, diagnosis and treatment of each patient. Having the previous day off was not an excuse.

Matron was wise to the student nurses trying to hide, however, and would march into the sluice room to find her prey—a student nurse.

We were all terrified of Matron, but although reluctant at first, I always ended up enjoying escorting her round the wards—and I learned a lot each time. Luckily, the patients were aware of how strict Matron was and often said their names, with a smile and a wink, to help us out.

One time the surgical ward was full; all 30 beds were occupied.

We had to take patients from casualty. The porters worked hard, collecting extra beds from the

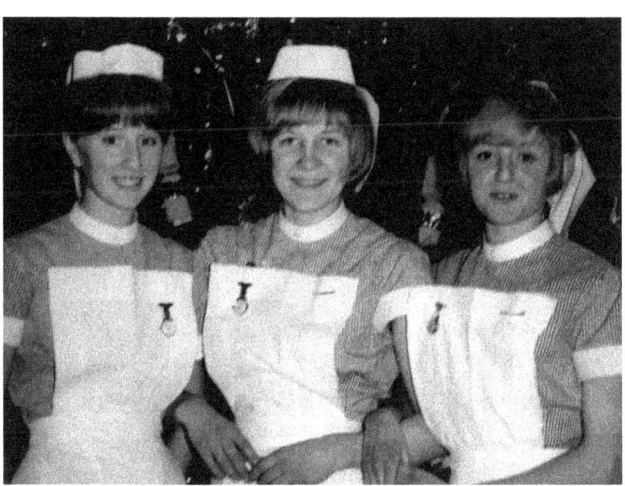

Top: working on Hannah Pickard Ward
Bottom: Christmas Day 1966, second-year students.

cellar storerooms. They were set up down the centre of the ward, with screens for privacy.

We never turned patients away nor left them on trolleys in the corridors.

Night Shifts

The night shift was not my favourite shift. I often struggled to stay awake on the bus home the following morning. Within minutes of the bus setting off, I was asleep.

The bus drivers were used to me and always asked where I wanted to be dropped off. The driver would wake me at my stop at Fitzwilliam.

The hospital was quite scary at night. I used to run through the corridors as fast as possible when transferring from wards. There was always a porter to jump out and frighten you.

Of course, there was talk about the hospital being haunted at night by Victorian nurses and dead patients. All quite untrue!

Not every patient slept at night. Some were confused, trying to climb out of bed over the metal sides. Some were extremely poorly and needed nursing care all night.

We had a desk in the middle of the ward with a small light to enable us to record our medical notes. It was quite scary, even on the wards, as patients would wander about, tapping you on the shoulder.

Night duty in casualty

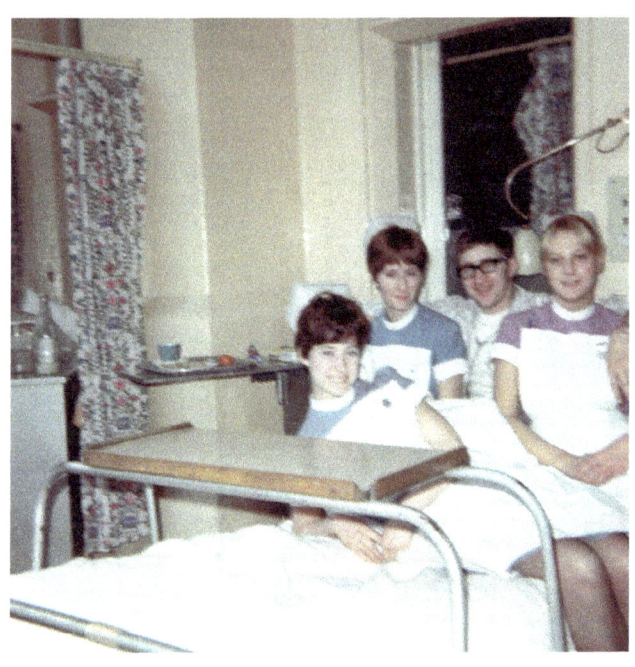

The male student nurse in bed following severe epistaxis

Often a patient requested a cup of tea and of course, within minutes, all 30 patients wanted one. I didn't mind; it was my job—and I loved it.

The worst part of night duty was when a patient died. The body had to be left in bed on the ward until the following morning, when the mortuary was open. I felt sorry for the rest of the patients, who often knew the patient had died.

One night I was in charge of the medical ward and working with a new male student nurse. It was going well, all patients were in bed by midnight. Then the male nurse suffered a nosebleed, quite a bad epistaxis. So off he went to casualty, leaving me alone to cope all night.

I carried on alone and the patients were helpful, knowing I was on my own. One hour later, the porter brought the student back in a wheelchair. He then occupied our only empty bed, with huge cotton-gauze pads protruding from his nose. Meanwhile, I worked all night without help.

The day staff arrived the following morning to see the male nurse in bed, and they found it highly amusing. I'm pleased to report that he made a full recovery.

We were taught the anatomy and physiology of every organ and structure in the body in preparation for our state finals, often performing practical procedures on each other and injecting oranges. We

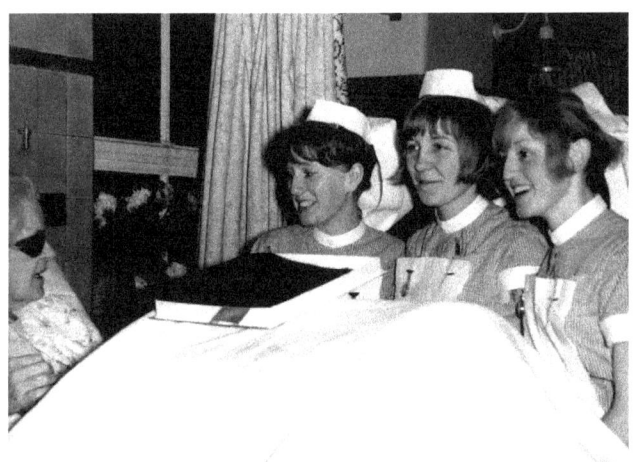

Working on the wards

had no plastic disposable syringes; we had to use reusable metal ones.

Working on placements brought theory and practise together. One was obstetric training at Manygates Hospital in Wakefield. The obstetric training lasted for 12 weeks, during which we learned about the nine-month gestation period and the delivery of babies.

This was an introduction to midwifery, and we were told that if any of us wished to train as a midwife, the three months would reduce the full midwifery training.

I was not intending to do that. I had my sights set on district nursing after I qualified. I had a vision of me on a bike with a black bag, riding around the village. How wrong was I!

Working in the maternity hospital opened my eyes to childbirth, and I assisted many deliveries. One traumatic birth saw a baby delivered with only one eye—most upsetting for the family and the staff.

I also worked on a premature-baby unit, feeding tiny babies which could fit in the palm of my hand. They were all nursed in incubators. I was to meet up with them again later in my career.

It was my last year of training, and I was beginning to feel confident and full of knowledge. The obstetric placement finished and I returned to Clayton Hospital ready for my next placement, which was on the medical ward. None of the nurses liked it there because of the notorious ward sister.

Working on the medical ward, I gained a lot of experience but it had its stressful days. I was working with one of the strictest of ward sisters, who loved having junior staff to control and enjoyed showing off her authority.

One day, I was feeding a patient lunch when I dropped the tray. It made such a loud clatter that the sister came out of her office on to the ward. She shouted at me across the ward, in front of all the patients and staff.

I was so upset that I had to take a few moments to compose myself in the kitchen. The kindly cook and cleaner gave me encouragement to carry on and return to the ward. I did, and a lovely elderly gentleman patient called me over to his bed.

"I saw what happened," he said, "and I want you to have this poem. I am 92 years old, and this poem has helped me through each day."

He was right. I love the poem. I have reflected on it many times and have passed it on to many people. Up to this day I can hear him saying it. It was just what I needed. God bless you.

> *It is easy enough to be pleasant,*
> *When life flows by like a song,*
> *But the man worthwhile is one who*

will smile,
When everything goes dead wrong.

(Extract from *Worth While* by Ella Wheeler Wilcox)

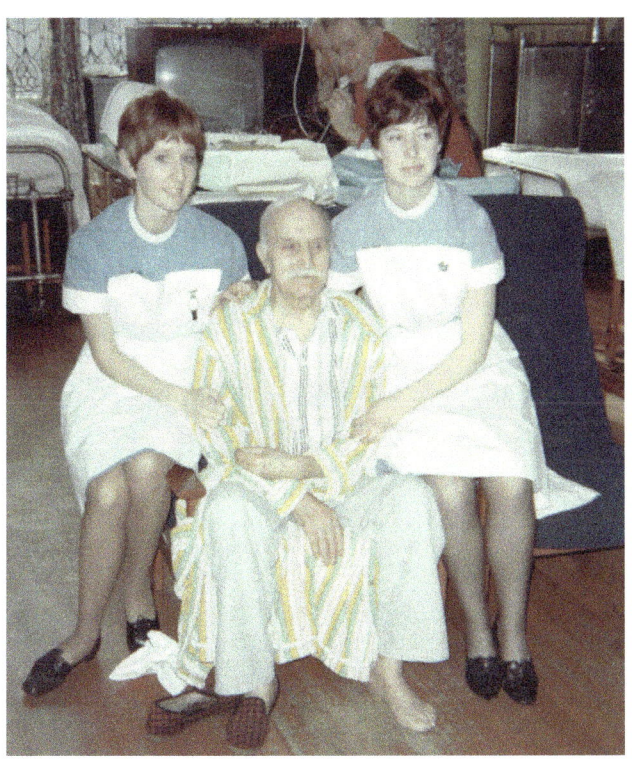

The poem was given to me by this gentleman.
I reflected on it many times

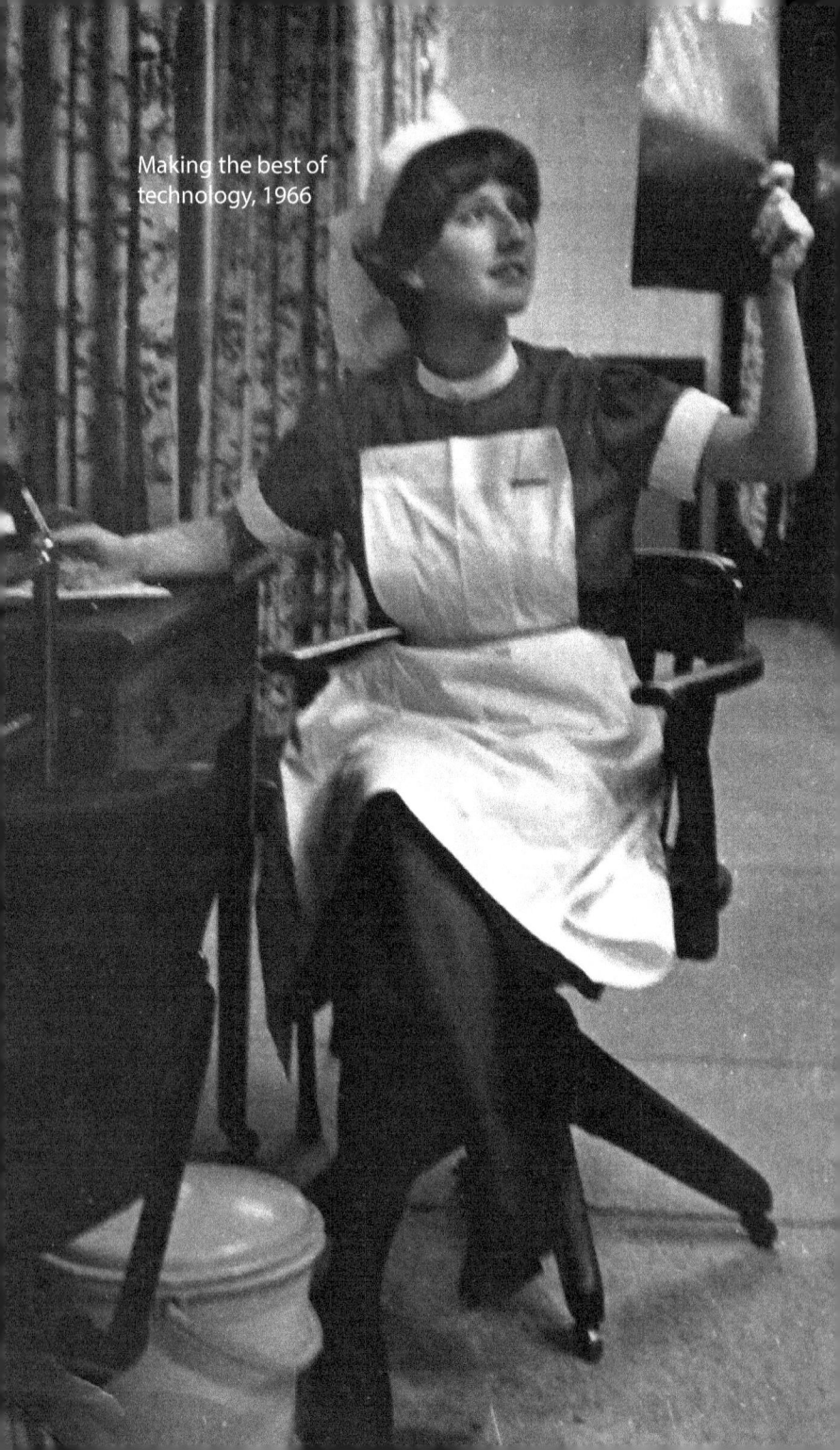

Making the best of technology, 1966

Technology

Over the 50 years of nursing, technology has moved on and it is now very different. In my training from 1964–1967 we had no computers to record patients' records; everything was recorded on paper and had to be legible and accurate. The doctors could have done with handwriting training though!

We had one telephone on the ward, in the sister's office. Patients didn't have phones or computers either. They had to wait until visiting time to talk to relatives. There was just one hour's visiting a day. Now it is open visiting on all wards.

X-rays and scans were limited and often unreadable. The print was very poor.

We often stayed over after shifts to update our nursing records. Legibility and confidentiality were priorities.

We spent a lot of time running up and down corridors to wards and laboratories for results. We had to go to the records department for patients' histories, which often took time. The lone ward telephone was always busy.

Sterilization and Autoclaving

The modern day NHS has changed for the better. We now have sterile-supplies departments to deliver all sterile packs for every procedure. When I was training, nights were the best time to sterilize

Using the autoclave to sterilize equipment

dressings and instruments. We had to wash bandages and dry them on the radiators. Patients would roll them up for us when dry.

We made packs of five cotton-wool balls and cut five-inch dressing squares from huge rolls of gauze. We had large metal drums to fill. Then we put them in the autoclave to sterilize.

All instruments were sterilized in the same way. It was extremely time consuming. This had to be carried out by night staff so that they were ready the following day.

Working in the operating theatre, I spent most of my time sterilizing equipment for operations. All gauze swabs had to be counted before and after operations to make sure that none were left inside the patient.

Theatre was interesting but sometimes stressful, particularly when children were involved.

I was young myself, only 18, and quickly had to cope as an adult.

I cried on my way home many times but was always ready to go back the next day.

Final Examination

My three years' nursing training seemed to pass very quickly.

In my third year, John and I decided to get married, which we did on 28 January 1967. We bought a terraced bungalow for £1,000 cash, which John's father lent to us.

I found it easier to revise for my finals with John helping me. We were ten students who started together. We all helped each other to revise. The exam date was pending and we knew that it was a big responsibility. Our tutors, family and friends, wanted us all to pass.

In 1967, all the nurses across the country took the same exam paper at the same time on the same day. The practical part was taken in the hospital training room with tutors and examiners. Patients from the wards acted as patients for the purpose of the exam. They were happy to help and tried to make us feel at ease.

We had to wait six agonising weeks for the results. When the letter finally dropped through the postbox, I couldn't open it; John had to do it. His big smiled told me I had passed. *Wow!* I immediately rang my parents. It was an amazing feeling. Three years' hard work had all been worth it. My parents were really proud.

In fact, all the nurses I had trained with had passed the exam, which made me even happier.

I continued to work at Clayton Hospital as a staff nurse to gain further experience. I still wanted to be a district nurse but felt I looked too young.

100 per cent success in S.R.N. exam

(O609R)

Eleven candidates trained at Wakefield Clayton Hospital who sat the General Nursing Council's examinations in October for the qualification of State Registered Nurse, all passed, thus enabling the hospital again to achieve a 100 per cent. success.

Final Examination: Hilary Fenn, Wakefield; Marjorie Milsom, Ossett; Sheila Pauline Ashford, Pontefract; Judith Sanderson, Ossett; Barbara Pickersgill, Ryhill; Jennifer Ann Rack, Wakefield; Patricia Ann Darbyshire, Wakefield.

Preliminary Examination, Part I and II: Mabel Franks, Oulton.

Preliminary Examination, Paart II only: Eileen Elizabeth Dorgana, Doncasater; Hilda June Kemp, Castleford; Janet May Orr, Doncaster.

NURSING SUCCESS

A former Fitzwilliam girl, Mrs Barbara Pickersgill (nee Padgett) was delighted to receive notice on Monday that she had passed her State Registered Nursing examination.

Barbara, who has been nursing at Clayton Hospital, Wakefield, for four years, is now living at 32, Sunny Bank, Ryhill, with her husband, Mr John Michael Pickersgill.

A former pupil at Kinsley Secondary School, she had an extra incentive to do well in the examination as she took it on her 21st birthday, October 10.

The youngest daughter of Mr and Mrs H. Padgett, of 2, George Street, Ryhill, she intends to carry on nursing at Clayton Hospital.

Mrs Pickersgill.

Local newspapers reported on our success

A night out to celebrate passing our exams.
Left to right: Marjorie Milson, Andrea Gillian, Judith Sanderson, Patricia Darbyshire & me

Prize giving 1968, held at Queen Elizabeth Grammar
School, Wakefield. All nurses, tutors, matrons
& the mayor were present

I enjoyed working in casualty, not knowing what I would face each day. There were a variety of conditions from cut fingers to major trauma.

One day, we had a call to say there was a road traffic accident coming in with three adults injured. There was no other information.

When the patients arrived, I was shocked to see they were my parents and sister. They had been travelling to Leeds to collect my sister's wedding dress when they had been involved in a car crash.

Fortunately, my mother had only a mild laceration to her leg. My father and sister were in shock but had no injuries. After treatment they were able to continue with their journey leaving me, greatly relieved, to carry on with my work.

Casualty was a good learning experience. I learned how to be calm and cope with all situations professionally. On Saturdays it was all football injuries; in the school holidays it was mainly children; at weekends and evenings it was alcohol-related injuries. We always had a porter on hand in case of disturbances.

I worked on the children's ward, which I loved. On operating days it was mainly tonsillectomies and appendectomies. The ward sister was extremely professional: she would not let staff have days off on operation day. Usually there would be ten children having their tonsils out on theatre days. Sister would allocate one nurse to one patient. The nurse would sit at the child's bedside and observe the child in case of any bleeding. One complication of a tonsillectomy could be bleeding, especially in redheads (like me). Sister always said that no child would have a complication on her ward.

The children's ward was next to the orthopaedic ward, where most of the patients were long-stay patients with fractures. So I used to take the children round to see these bedfast patients, as we called them. The children would sit on the beds and play with the bedfast patients. It was good for morale as some of the orthopaedic patients had children, whom they were missing.

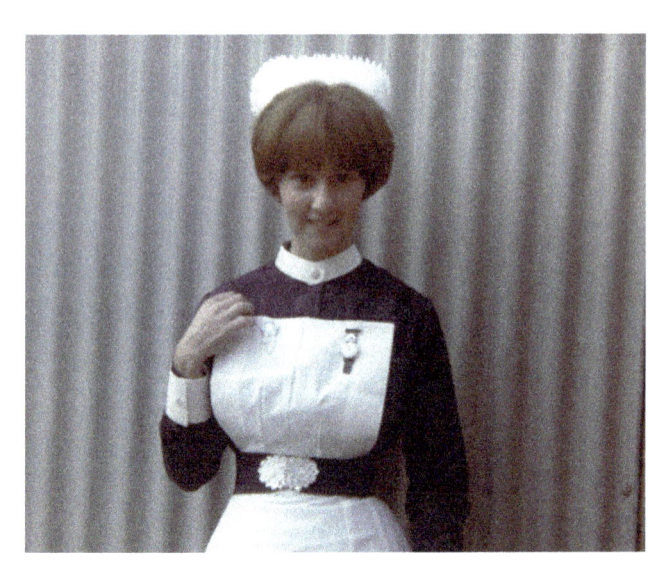

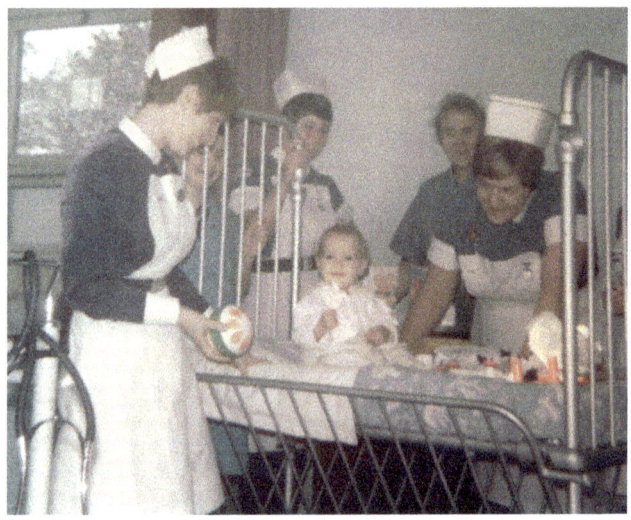

Top: my first sister's post, Snapethorpe Hospital, 1969
Bottom: Snapethorpe Hospital's 12-cubicle infectious diseases ward

IV
My First Sister's Post

It was time to move on, and a post was advertised for a junior ward sister at Snapethorpe Hospital, Wakefield, which I applied for. I was successful.

It was a 12-cubicle ward, where infectious-diseases patients were cared for, mainly children with a few adults. I was looking forward to starting my new post.

Wearing my new sister's uniform I felt proud, as did my parents and John. There was a senior sister in charge of the 12-bed unit. The consultant came from Seacroft Hospital to carry out a ward round twice weekly and to prescribe treatments.

Some of the children and babies were seriously dehydrated with gastro-enteritis. Sadly, we were unable to save them all, which was heartbreaking.

The children were nursed in individual cubicles because of infection—salmonella, E. coli, gastro-enteritis and infectious diseases like measles, scarlet fever, whooping cough. We had a lot of dehydrated Asian babies, and all the families would arrive to see them, sometimes as many as 20 visiting one child.

While I was at Snapethorpe, the Manygates Hospital's premature-baby unit suffered a salmonella outbreak. This meant the ward had to be evacuated ready for disinfecting and cleaning down. The only place with cubicles suitable was our 12-cubicle unit at Snapethorpe.

I was very happy to see the babies come to our unit and pitched in to help. We were set up with all the equipment and incubators to take the babies. I remembered all the training I had with premature babies from my obstetrics training at Manygates.

The staff from Manygates also came to help look after the babies and give their expertise. Four weeks we looked after the babies. I loved having them. We were all sad to see them return to Manygates.

I returned back to the infectious-diseases unit and continued my work there. It felt good to have been allowed to accommodate the premature babies. In fact, it felt good to help all our children to improve and eventually go home. We had a lot of whooping cough and measles, very ill children. Hopefully we have improved that now with immunisation.

My Moment of Stardom

It was while I was working at Snapethorpe Hospital that I had my moment of stardom.

I was quite excited to hear that I had been selected to help with promoting sterile dressing packs. These were quite new to nursing, and it was a novelty to have sterile dressing packs—no more washing bandages and drying them on the radiators!

The advertising company came to the ward to set up its cameras.

I had to perform a dressing on a child while they filmed, using their products. My little patient performed perfectly as I had done his dressing many times and he was used to me doing it.

Apparently the poster was to be used on displays all around the country at nursing events.

I felt very privileged to have been asked, and I felt like a star for the day.

I continued working on the infectious diseases unit for a few years and enjoyed every day of it.

It was from Snapethorpe Hospital that I left to have my daughter, Lisa. After three months I started back on the unit, part-time, for a short period.

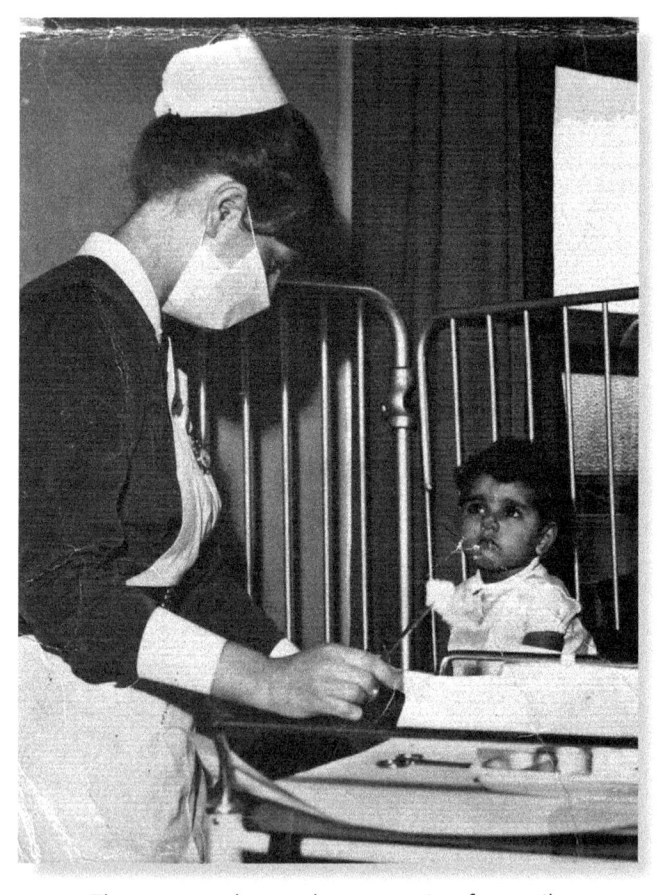

This page and next: the promotion for sterile
dressing packs starring yours truly

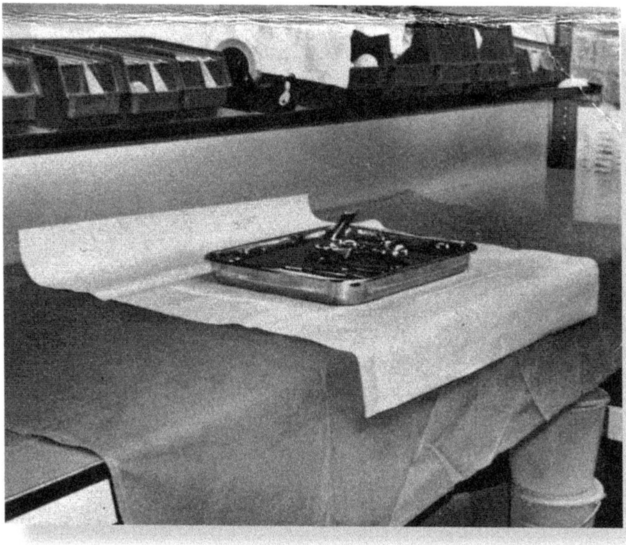

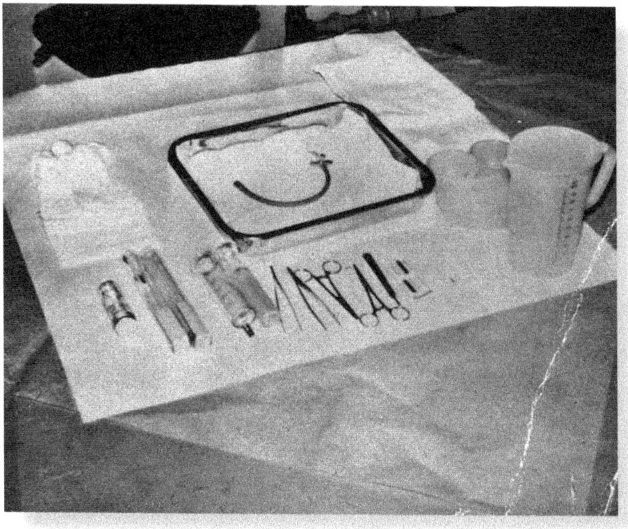

12 years after starting nurse training, my dream came true: I became a district nurse. The health authority had a lease car scheme. The amount was deducted from our wages each month. We were able to change the car every three years. It cost an average of £80–100 per month

V
District Nursing

I applied for, and was successful in getting, a district-nursing post working for Wakefield and Pontefract East Division health authority. The date was 1 June 1976. It was a dream come true.

My contract was for 40 hours a week on a salary of £3,864 per year (around £30,000 today).

I worked as a relief sister for a while, visiting patients in their homes, giving nursing care and treatments. I also had to relieve other district nurses while they took annual leave. So I gained good knowledge of the local areas, from Wakefield out to Hemsworth, West Yorkshire.

To become a team leader and community caseload manager, I had to do further training. So I signed up for a district-nurse training course at Bradford College. It was six months' training with a placement in the community. At the end of the training, I passed the examination and became a qualified district nurse.

This was what I had wanted since the start of my career. After working as a relief sister for a while, a caseload-manager post became available covering Havercroft, my home village.

I applied and was fortunate to be successful.

The practice was in its early days, with new, young GPs (general practitioners) as well as a brand new building.

I was my own team leader, looking after a caseload of 6–7,000 patients. I decided who needed a visit on any given day. Morning insulin injections were a priority.

I became well known in the area and built up friendships and trust within the community. I also held clinic sessions daily at the health centre for patients who were mobile.

The two practice GPs gave me new patients to visit on a daily basis. After my first visit, I would decide how often they needed further visits.

The practice grew over the years and the patient list expanded. Eventually, as work became busier, a nursing auxiliary was taken on to help me. Her role was visiting patients and assisting them with bathing. She was known in the village as 'the bath nurse.' The trust also gave me a staff nurse to help with the workload.

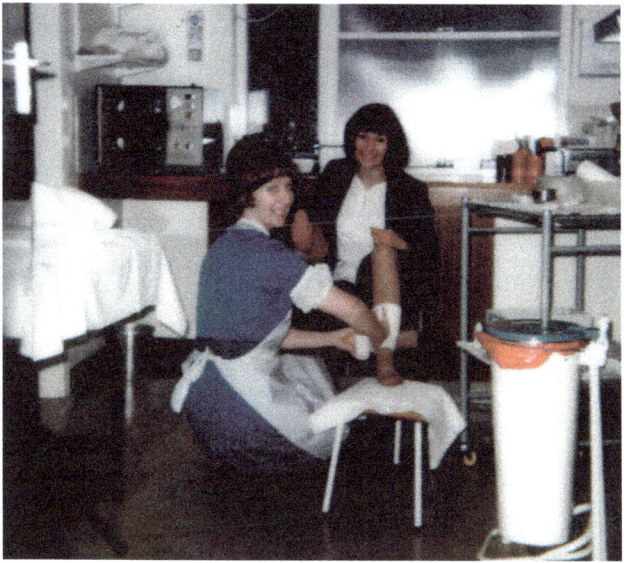

Top: with the receptionist
Bottom: clinic sessions at Havercroft health centre

One bonus of the job was
meeting patients' pets

Patients' Pets

Dogs are not always man's best friend—especially when it comes to district nurses.

I am an animal lover and enjoyed meeting most of the family pets. On some occasions, however, they were not so friendly.

My doctor referred one patient to me to assess what support and nursing care was required. I knocked at the patient's door. It was a small bungalow. I could hear the dog barking behind the door and the lady inside shouting at the dog.

Looking through the window, I could see that the lady was in a wheelchair, beckoning me to come in as the door was open.

"Is the dog safe?" I asked.

"Oh yes. Come in."

Slowly I opened the door. The dog, a Jack Russell, was barking and snarling and showing me her teeth. I put my foot through the door to ease her away, when she sunk her teeth into my ankle. Immediately I closed the door, walked round to the window and told the lady I would telephone her. I returned to the surgery to wash the bite wound, and one of my colleagues gave me a tetanus injection.

I still had the patient to assess, but the dog was out of her control.

Checking the patient's records, I found the address and phone number of her son, who arranged

One of the health visitors in our professional team

to meet me—with the dog put away. I was then able to conduct my assessment successfully.

On another occasion, I visited a patient's house, one of those where the three-piece suite was on the outside of the house (in the front garden) instead of inside. I could hear a dog inside, and I reluctantly knocked on the door. I could see the huge dog, barking and jumping at the glass door. I opened the letter box to be greeted by two very large eyes and then a huge tongue protruding through it.

A man shouted through the locked door, "Who is it?"

I answered that it was the district nurse.

He replied, very abruptly, "Go away before I set the dog on you."

Well I didn't need telling twice, so I retreated quickly. I never went back.

We had a good nursing team, with me as caseload manager. Every day was busy: visiting patients in their homes and giving treatments, dressings, injections and nursing care.

The patients were generally happy to see us as often we were the only people they saw all day.

We had other professionals working at the health centre: midwives, physiotherapists, occupational therapists, a GP and the clerical team. We worked as a professional team, giving a holistic approach to nursing care.

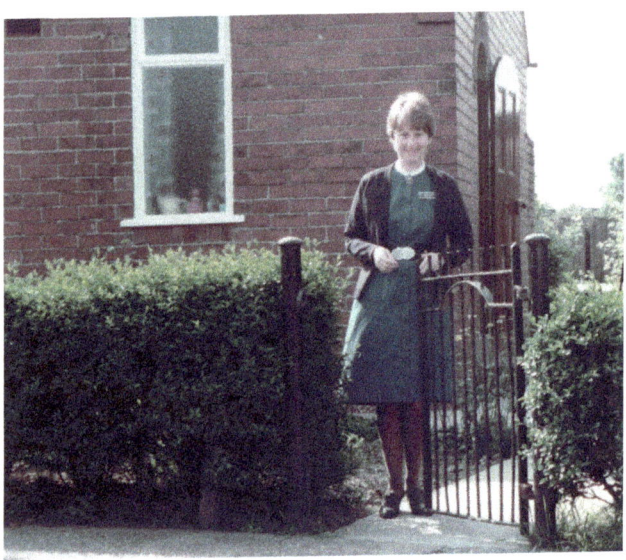

We had to work in all weather conditions, even when the roads were blocked with snow. We would walk to the more urgent patients & reduced our workload until the weather improved

I worked for the practice over a period of 25 years. I continued to update my skills and training. There was always more to learn. I enrolled on a training course at Bradford College to become a practical-work teacher. This would mean I could mentor, and teach, new district nurses under my care.

I also went on to study the nurse prescribing course at Sheffield University. There was an extensive textbook to work through. I finished the course and passed the exam.

This was a big move forward for nurses. We were able to prescribe items for patients without them having to see the doctor. It was a limited list: dressings, bandages, urinary products, all the items we would need to give nursing care. It was carefully monitored, but, as nurses, we knew the costs of each item.

We never knew what to expect in a day's work. What I had planned for my visits on a particular day often didn't happen. One day my GP, Dr Rashid, asked me to visit a patient to give him a tetanus injection. The patient had fallen in the garden and had a minor laceration to his hand.

Dr Rashid had left a prescription for the tetanus ampoule, which his wife was due to collect from the local chemist. I arrived at the patient's house to administer the injection but found they were not expecting me. The patient's wife explained that she had broken open the ampoule and given her husband the liquid in a teaspoon. It was not supposed to be swallowed. I rang the GP to explain, and he wanted the patient to be transferred to casualty for a stomach washout. So, from a minor injury in the garden, the patient was having a stressful procedure, performed in casualty. Happily he did make a full recovery, and I visited the next day, when we reflected on the incident with some amusement.

We had no mobile phones, and often visited patients we had not met before, so safety was always on my mind.

I visited one elderly gentleman to syringe his ears as he was suffering from hearing loss. While I was there, he asked me to fill his coal buckets from the cellar. It was a mining village. Everyone had coal fires.

I went down to the cellar and started to fill his bucket, when the patient closed and locked the cellar door. I realised he had forgotten I was down there. Unfortunately, due to his deafness, he could not hear me knocking on the cellar door. I was there for three hours until the meals-on-wheels lady arrived and heard me calling for help!

It made me late for the rest of my calls, but it was a lesson learned and an amusing story for my colleagues.

There were many incidents over the 25-year period, some amusing, others not so amusing.

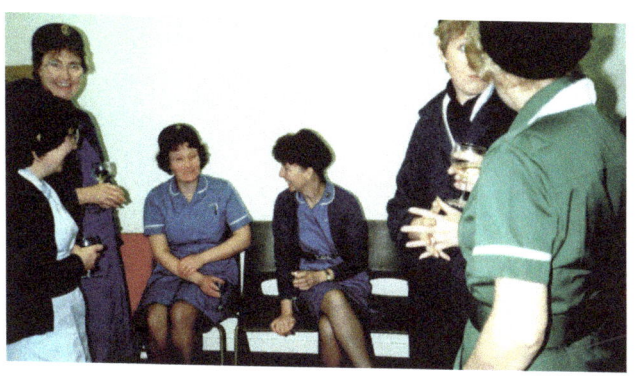

A monthly meeting with other district nurses. The health authority wanted all the nursing staff to have regular updates and provided training days. When we had professional meetings, we often invited representatives to demonstrate new products coming into use. We would also say goodbye to staff who were leaving

I lived in the village where I worked and the villagers knew me well. There were many people who knocked on my door to ask for help with road accidents, collapses and just for advice. It was usually when I was off duty. I was always willing to help, though. After all, that was what I had trained for.

While on my daily rounds, I often met the pets of patients, not just dogs. When visiting one young girl to remove her sutures after an appendectomy, she looked at me and said, very distressed, "Will you please look at my foal?"

We went to the stables. The adorable little horse had a badly cut leg. The girl had rung the vet, but he could not come out for two days. She was very worried about infection to the open wound.

I cleaned the wound and applied a dressing, securing it with a bandage while the foal's mother looked on. This was my first time treating a horse, but the procedure was the same as with a human.

A few weeks later, I saw the little foal running around the field. So all was well; the foal made a full recovery.

Once, my husband and I were travelling home from a week's holiday in Tenerife. It was our 25th wedding anniversary. We were enjoying a meal on the plane when there was a call over the loud speaker: *Is there a doctor on board?*

No one responded. We looked at each other before I called the air hostess over.

"I am not a doctor, but I am a nurse and I may be able to help."

It was a young girl, just 20 years old, having difficulty breathing and very distressed, as was her partner who was sitting with her. It was obvious to me that she was hyperventilating. It can sometimes occur on a flight, which some people find stressful.

I asked her to breathe into a paper bag. Panic attacks are caused by too much oxygen. Breathing into a paper bag slowly helps you to re-inhale carbon monoxide. It seems strange but it does really work believe it or not.

I sat with her and talked through the process over the next two hours. When we eventually landed, the paramedics took her to hospital in Leeds for a check-up. The captain thanked me for my help and said it had saved one of the air hostesses having to sit with her. I was just happy she did not deteriorate on the flight.

The staff offered me two bottles of duty free as a thank you. I said no thank you, I was just happy to help. I later received a lovely letter from Monarch Airlines thanking me for what I had done.

I had worked for 25 years as a district nurse in Havercroft. My daughter had grown up and was married with her own son, our beautiful grandson.

The letter that Monarch Airlines sent to me

My husband and I had a desire to live near the sea at that time. It was time to reduce my hours. We decided to move to Bridlington, where I hoped to continue as a district nurse, part-time.

I was given a wonderful send-off by the staff and friends at the health centre. Many patients came to thank me for all the care I had given, and I received 11 bouquets from patients and friends.

Popular nurse retires

by Peter Jordan
peterjordan&wakefieldexpress.co.uk

POPULAR nursing Sister Barbara Pickersgill found herself bowled over with bouquets from colleagues and patients at her retirement presentation at Havercroft Health Centre.

Mrs Pickersgill and her husband John have become very popular with people using the centre or receiving home visits during the past 25 years.

Born in Fitzwilliam, Mrs Pickersgill used to be a regular at the centre on Cow Lane before it became her work place as was previously used for holding dances.

She started as a cadet nurse at Wakefield Clayton Hospital in 1962 and later completed her staff nurse training.

After her marriage the couple lived at South Hiendley and after the birth of daughter Lisa, Mrs Pickersgill trained as a district nurse and joined the new Havercroft Health Centre in 1976.

She has had a large area to cover, stretching from Shafton, Cudworth and Grimethorpe to Walton and Crofton, along with South Hiendley, Ryhill, Havercroft, Hemsworth, Kinsley and Fitzwilliam.

Husband John, who was also employed in the Health Service, helped on many occasions to answer emergency calls, while Mrs Pickersgill also introduced a number of new services at the centre.

Mrs Pickersgill received 11 bouquets and she will use the cheque she was awarded to buy a Winchester Napoleon clock

She is also an excellent cake maker and icer, and has created the cake for their daughter's wedding in Scotland next month. The couple has moved to live at Bridlington.

FOND farewell: Dr Dar, of Havercroft Health Centre, presents Mrs Pickersgill with a bouquet watched by her husband John h0684b144

My retirement made it into the local paper!

With colleagues when I retired

VI
Nursing at the Seaside

I managed to secure employment at Bessingby Hall nursing home in Bridlington while waiting for a district-nurse post to become available. It was a private nursing home, not what I was used to, but I enjoyed the work nonetheless.

After a few months' working there, one of the community nurses told me that a district nurse was leaving her post and the position was to be advertised.

I rang her manager, who asked me to attend an interview. I was accepted and started work two weeks later.

I was based at Bridlington Hospital with other district nurses. Each GP practice was allocated a district nurse to work with them. Mine was a good surgery called Manor House. It had four GPs, all of whom I got on with very well.

For the next six years I worked in Bridlington, visiting patients in their homes, nursing homes, and the many caravan parks in the area. We also ran a minor-injuries clinic for patients and holidaymakers at Bridlington Hospital, which was open daily from 10am to 12pm.

In the school holidays, we walked the beaches, giving advice about sunburn and offering free sunscreen lotion samples. This was great fun, and I thoroughly enjoyed it.

There were often terminally ill patients who were staying in caravans for the summer season. We gave them full nursing care, providing everything they needed.

The nursing side is the same wherever you are, but the environment was different at Bridlington.

I enjoyed my time working there, but after eight years' in Bridlington, my daughter was expecting her second child and we decided to move back to West Riding.

John and I sold our home and I said goodbye to all my colleagues and friends.

We bought a bungalow at Pollington, a few miles from my daughter. I continued to be a grandream, looking after the children for a few months. However, I was soon ready to return to work again, part-time.

Top: my leaving party at Bridlington with the nursing staff
Bottom: Monument House rehabilitation unit. Celebrating Kate Middleton & Prince William's wedding day on 29 April 2011. All the patients watched the event with us

VII
Bevan Ward & Monument House Rehabilitation Units

I applied and was successful in gaining a position as a staff nurse on a new unit being opened at Pontefract Hospital, Bevan Ward. It was a 25-bed rehabilitation unit.

Patients were transferred from the wards to the unit for rehabilitation before being discharged home. On the unit were medical doctors, nurses, auxiliary staff and a physiotherapy team.

Patients were assessed on admission and given a plan of care for their rehabilitation. The average stay was three to four weeks.

After two years, the health authority wanted to provide more rehabilitation beds, with one unit in Wakefield and one in Pontefract. The Bevan Ward was to be demolished, so we were moved to Monument House, one mile from the hospital. The care and treatment were the same, just on different premises. The trust opened the rehabilitation unit in Wakefield, at Queen Elizabeth House, and I worked there too.

VIII
Queen Elizabeth House

The new rehabilitation unit had more beds available. Patients came from local hospitals in the area: Pinderfields, Pontefract and Dewsbury. The unit was busy and always full. All the professionals worked as a team to rehabilitate patients so that they could return home into the community.

Consultants came twice weekly to the unit to assess patients and provide treatment. The nursing staff were responsible for the management of care and giving the medications. The main referrals came from the new Pinderfields hospital.

We were based just in the grounds, not in the main hospital building. This often led to confusion as people did not think we were part of the NHS trust. We had to explain on many occasions that we were part of Wakefield and Pontefract NHS Trust after all.

Queen Elizabeth House rehabilitation unit

Filming for the Channel 4 documentary

My daughter, Lisa, worked on the unit as medical secretary. It was becoming a family affair!

While working at Queen Elizabeth House, Channel 4 were making a documentary about a patient we had on the ward. They were following his story through his illness and had filmed the patient over at Pinderfields Hospital in the weeks before.

They asked if they could film a nurse on our unit performing a dressing change with the patient. Well, I was nominated to be that nurse. After almost 50 years, I thought I could perform a dressing change!

It was quite stressful but turned out well and was shown as part of the documentary. The patient continued to improve and his wound healed. He was then discharged home with all the facilities in place to aid his rehabilitation there.

Meeting HRH Princess Royal

It was coming up to my 50 years' service with the NHS. I was invited to attend the opening ceremony of Pinderfields Hospital and be introduced to Anne, Princess Royal. I was delighted and excited to be asked. Other people were invited too, from many disciplines.

We had to be in place at the hospital in good time. Security were walking round, checking everywhere. The Princess Royal arrived on time with her lady-in-waiting and other officials.

We all stood in a line as she slowly made her way along. She shook my hand with a smile and asked what my job involved. She was very knowledgeable about the hospital. Someone told her that I had 50 years' service and seemed to be impressed. The princess then gave a speech officially opening the new hospital.

It was a lovely highlight to my career.

Official opening by The Princess Royal of the new Pinderfields Hospital, 13 September 2011

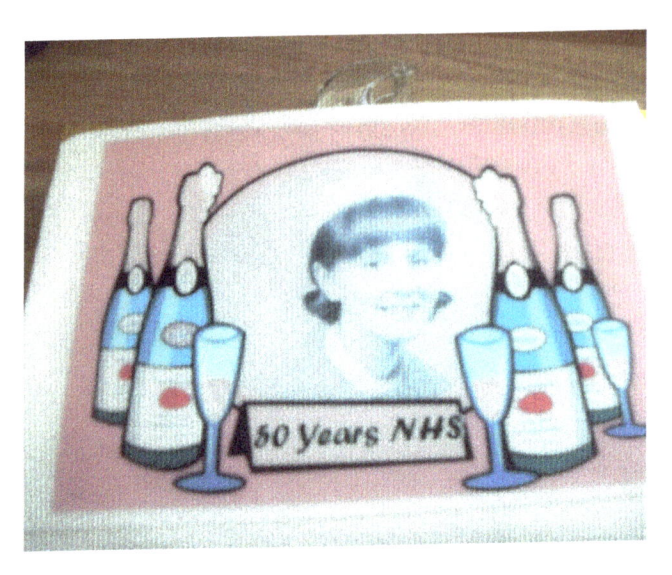

Retirement party, January 2015

IX
Retirement, January 2015

Well, my final day had arrived. I had mixed feelings about leaving. 50 years is a long time and I knew I would miss working.

I have worked with some wonderful colleagues and made lifetime friends. It's also been a great pleasure to meet all the wonderful patients I have nursed.

There were very sad occasions and I cried with families along the way. There were also many rewarding and happy times, which gave me the enthusiasm to carry on.

I have thoroughly enjoyed being a nurse, helping people to recover and cope with life.

I have to thank the NHS for giving me the training to cope with life and illness, also all the skills to be able to pass on to others. I will always be a nurse, caring for people until my last day. I was very sad to be retiring but, who knows, maybe one day I will return. It's been amazing!

© 2018 Barbara Pickersgill, RGN, PWT, NP, DNC

Lightning Source UK Ltd.
Milton Keynes UK
UKHW05f1347290518
323387UK00009B/106/P